Clifford Phonics Fun
Reading Program — Book 1: y, ey

Jetta Says Sorry

by Janelle Cherrington

Illustrated by Robin Cuddy

Based on the books by Norman Bridwell

SCHOLASTIC INC.
New York   Toronto   London   Auckland   Sydney
Mexico City   New Delhi   Hong Kong   Buenos Aires

It was animal week.

All week, the class would learn about animals.

Miss Carrington asked each child to bring in a stuffed animal.

Emily Elizabeth went first.

She had a funny little puppy.

It had a red body, floppy ears, and a big, happy smile.

"It looks like Clifford when he was a puppy," Emily Elizabeth said.

"ANIMAL WEEK"

Jetta went next.

"This is my pretty bunny, Lily," she began.

"As you can see, she has pink, fluffy ears. She has a really puffy tail.
And she has a basket for candy."

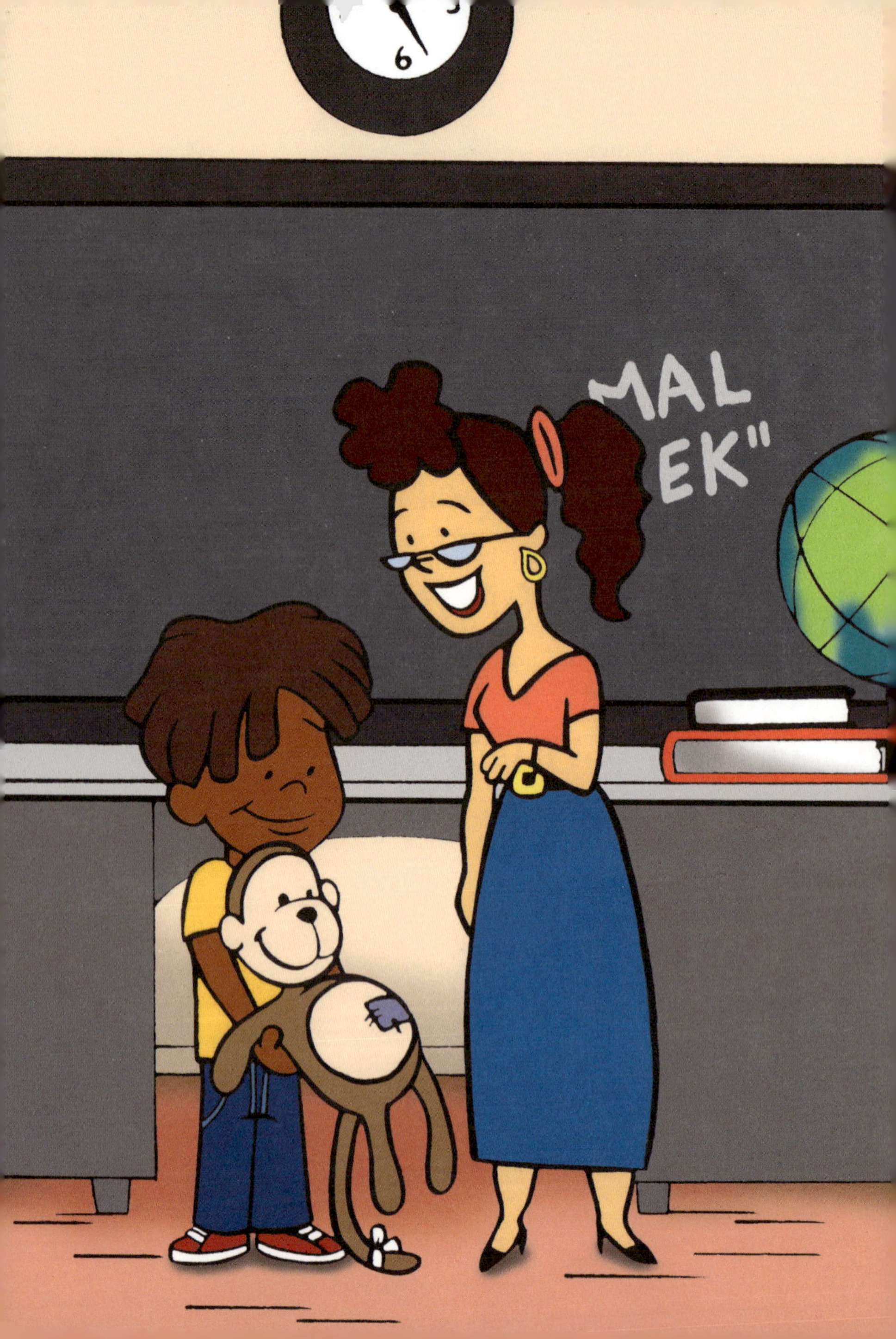
MAL
EK"

Charley went last.

He had a stuffed monkey.

It was old and ripped,
but it had a happy face
and a soft, floppy body.

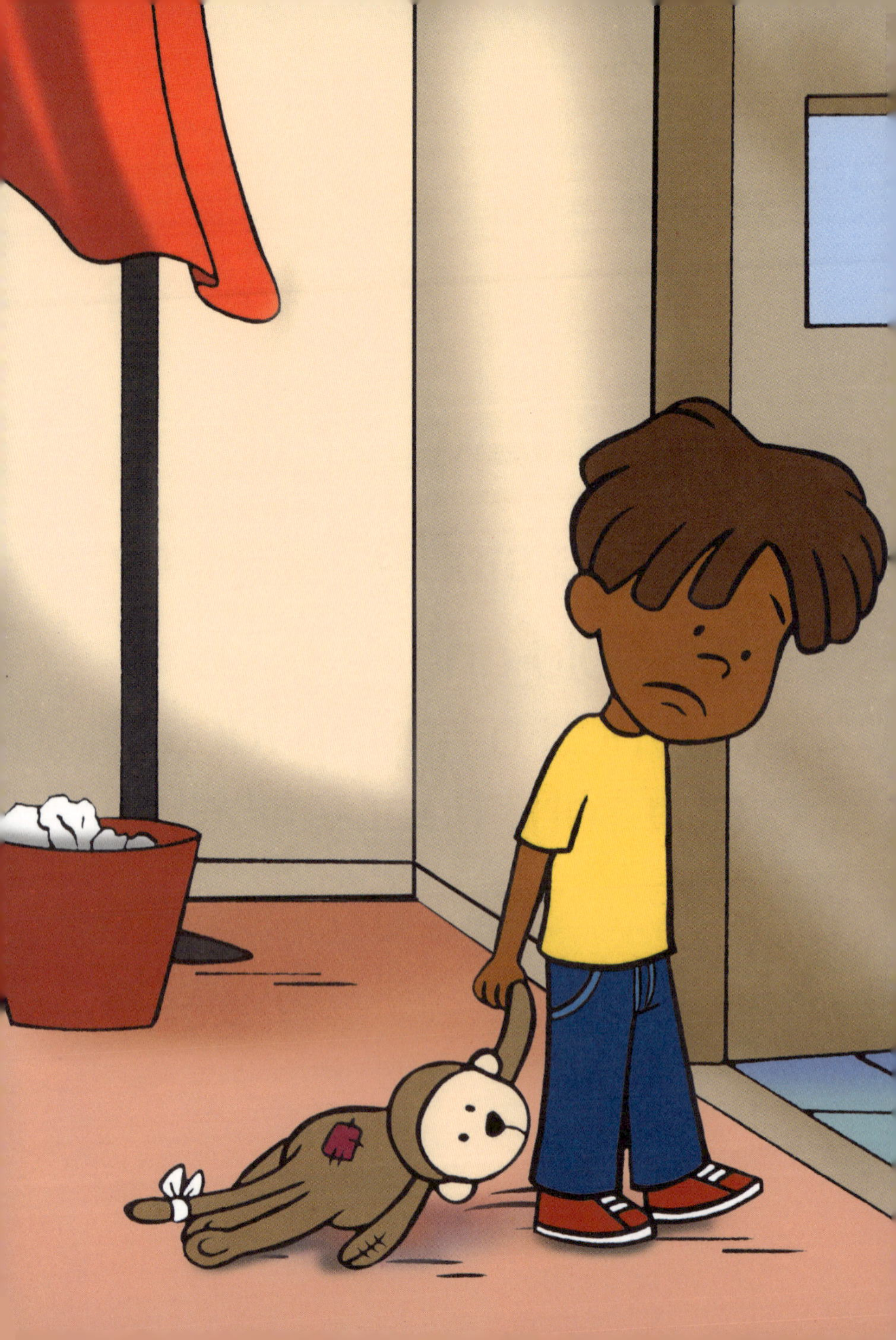

Most of the class liked the monkey.

But Jetta said, "Why did you bring that? It looks messy and ripped."

"It is old," Charley said. "It was my mom's."

Charley seemed sad.

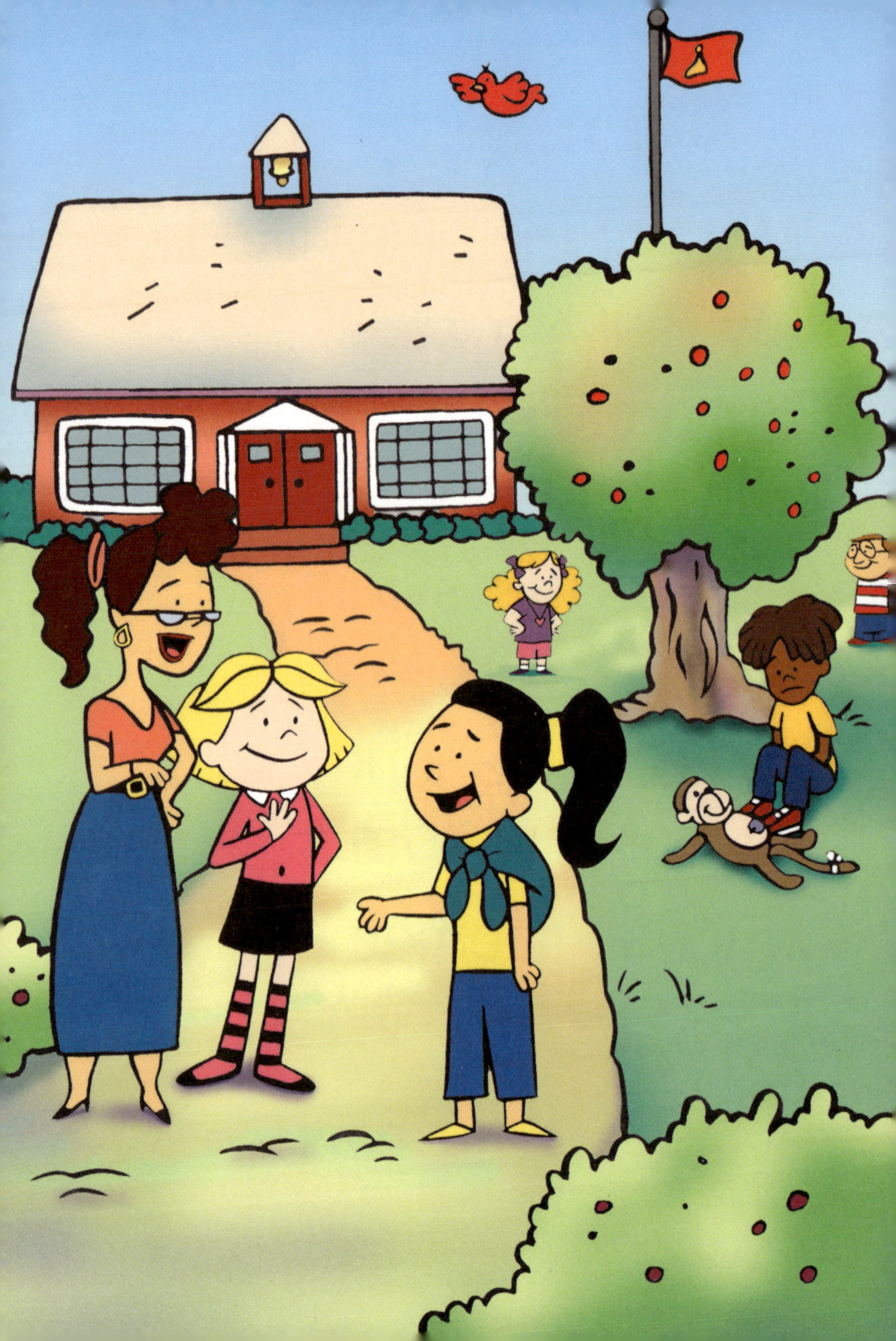

"You hurt his feelings," Emily Elizabeth said.

"I did?" Jetta said. "But I didn't mean to! What can I do?"

"You can say you're sorry," Miss Carrington said.

When Charley came back, Jetta said she was very, very sorry.

"What I said was not nice," she said.

"Your monkey is cute."

"Thanks," Charley said.

Charley felt better
and so did Jetta.